HELLO, MELBOURNE!

MEGAN McKEAN

Thames & Hudson

Good morning, MELBOURNE!
And good morning to YOU!

We magpies love living here.
After all, Melbourne has been
voted best city in the world!

Songbirds like us fit right in with all the music, theatre and arts.

Come and explore some of our favourite places. There are six of us to spot along the way.

Many Melburnians start their day with a train ride. Flinders Street is Australia's busiest station and the only one with a secret ballroom!

People meet under the clocks on the steps of the station. From here, you can watch our world-famous trams passing by.

FLINDERS STREET ST

Over the road is Federation Square, home of the Koorie Heritage Trust. There, you can see the art and culture of our Indigenous people.

Nearby is ACMI, a museum of gaming, cinema, computers and TV. You can learn about claymation, or even make a short film.

The National Gallery of Victoria is Australia's oldest and biggest art gallery. Its Great Hall has the world's largest stained-glass ceiling.

The water wall is our favourite, though the ducks prefer the moat. Can you see them splashing around?

A long time ago, a famous painting by Pablo Picasso was stolen. Nobody noticed for two days!

The painting was later returned, undamaged, but the thieves were never caught. Can you spot the naughty robbers?

The Royal Botanic Gardens are a great place to fly around. Lots of Melburnians like to jog along the Tan or picnic by the lake.

Some pay their respects at the Shrine of Remembrance. Others visit the Children's Garden and get their hands dirty!

You can also explore La Trobe's cottage. Victoria's first governor, Charles, squeezed into it with his wife Sophie and their four little La Trobes.

Today's governor lives in a grand mansion – Government House. If you can see the flag flying then the governor is at home.

Melbourne's colourful alleys and laneways are decorated with murals, stencils and graffiti.

Hosier Lane is one of the best. Different artists paint new pictures on the walls all the time.

It's like an ever-changing street art gallery. But the best artists like to paint us magpies.

Maybe one day there'll be a whole mural of us for you to enjoy!

Hop on the free heritage tram to the State Library. It's a great place to find bookworms – yum!

They come here to read some of the two million or so books in the library. But we like the different exhibitions best.

You'll find Ned Kelly's armour on display. He's Australia's most famous bushranger.

Nearby is the Old Melbourne Gaol, where Ned was locked up. You can explore the tiny gaol cells or dress up in a copy of his armour.

All this travelling has made us hungry. Let's stop for lunch at the Queen Victoria Market.

There are always good things to eat at the Queen Vic. We try something new each time.

For dessert, we enjoy a treat from
the famous hot doughnut van.
Can you see us making a mess?

You can also shop for souvenirs,
clothes, flowers or toys –
there's heaps to see and do!

Let's go and see a show at the
beautiful Princess Theatre.
The matinee is about to start.

Ballets, musicals, dramas and operas
have been performed here for over 150
years. There's even a resident ghost!

Opera singer Frederick Federici died before the end of a show, but the cast all saw him take a bow with them.

Can you spot Mr Federici in evening dress ready to watch this performance?

It's raining. Hop on a tram to Bourke Street Mall in the heart of the city and visit the Royal Arcade.

There, two giants, Gog and Magog, strike a bell each hour to tell Melburnians the time.

Keep walking and you'll find the Block Arcade, based on a grand arcade in Melbourne's sister city – Milan, Italy.

Let's have afternoon tea at the Hopetoun Tea Rooms. They've served tea and cakes since 1892.

Southbank is a great spot to spend an afternoon strolling beside the Yarra.

You can chug down the river in a steamboat or enjoy buskers performing along the bank.

In the Arts Centre you can see the ballet, listen to opera, or go to the theatre or a concert.

If you're lucky you might hear us magpies singing our favourite song!

The dad of famous singer
Dame Nellie Melba built the
Royal Exhibition Building.

He wanted to show
how grand Victoria was
after the gold rush.

Next door is Melbourne Museum, where you can see dinosaur and whale skeletons.

There's also Phar Lap, the famous racehorse. You can even feed the Museum's eels.

Let's head up to Lygon Street for dinner. We're starving. Do you feel like pizza or pasta? Or maybe both?

You'll find lots of delicious Italian food in Lygon Street, the heart of Melbourne's 'Little Italy'.

In spring each year, Lygon Street is closed off for a festival to celebrate all things Italian.

You can listen to music, or enjoy a treat from Australia's first gelati shop – just don't forget to share it with us!

It's fun to catch a game at the Melbourne Cricket Ground. In summer there's cricket and in winter, football.

The famous 'G is Australia's largest stadium and even hosted the Olympics in 1956.

The stands are packed with fans cheering on their favourite team during the football grand final.

If you see a footy team in black and white jumpers, that's Collingwood. They're named after us – the Magpies!

St Kilda is the most popular beach in Melbourne, with sea baths and Luna Park!

Nearby there are galleries, markets, theatres, gardens and lots of cake shops.

St Kilda Pier has a famous pavilion, but did you know, there's also a penguin colony?

If you wait until dusk, you might spot some little penguins coming home for the night.

We come home to the
Collingwood Children's Farm to
spend the night with our furred
and feathered friends.

During the day you can pat a pig,
feed the chooks, or learn how to
milk a cow. You might even spot
a gaggle of geese!

We like to join in the evening chorus of clucks and moos and chirps and barks. None of the others can sing like us, but they try.

We've had a wonderful day exploring our city with you. Good night, MELBOURNE. And good night to YOU!

For Joshua

First published in Australia in 2017
by Thames & Hudson Australia Pty Ltd
11 Central Boulevard Portside Business Park
Port Melbourne Victoria 3207
ABN: 72 004 751 964

www.thamesandhudson.com.au

20 19   5 4 3

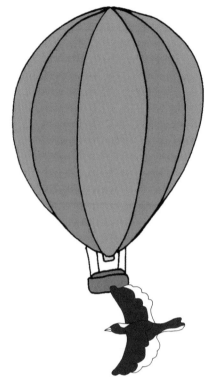

ISBN: 978 0 5005010 8 5

National Library of Australia Cataloguing-in-Publication entry
        Hello, Melbourne! / Megan McKean
        9780500501085 (hardback)
        Melbourne (Vic.)–Juvenile literature.
        Melbourne (Vic.)–Pictorial works.
        McKean, Megan, author, illustrator.

Design: Megan McKean
Editing: Nan McNab
Printed and bound in China by 1010.

Did you spot these different trams? See how many you can find next time you're in Melbourne.

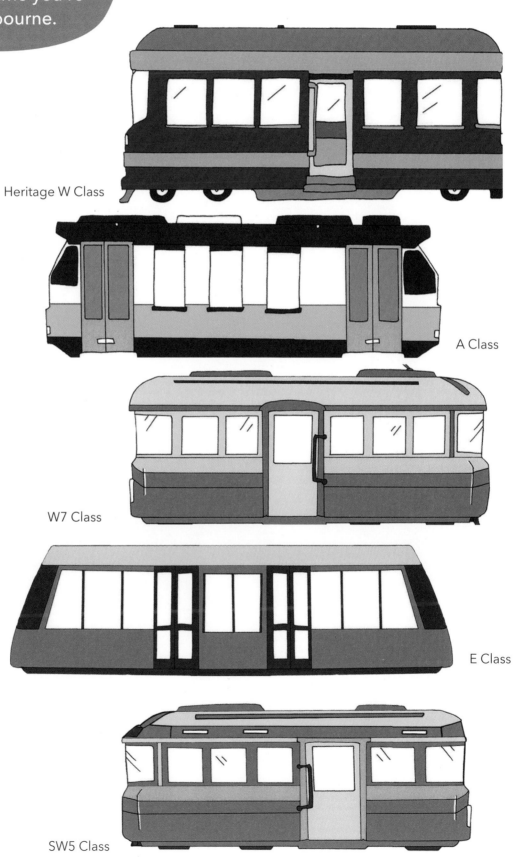

Heritage W Class

A Class

W7 Class

E Class

SW5 Class